# YOUR KNOWLEDGE HAS VALUE

**Swetha Reddy Allam, Kotagiri Santhosh**

# Survey on Distributed Data Mining Systems

GRIN Publishing

**Bibliographic information published by the German National Library:**

The German National Library lists this publication in the National Bibliography; detailed bibliographic data are available on the Internet at http://dnb.dnb.de .

**Imprint:**

Copyright © 2014 GRIN Verlag GmbH
Print and binding: Books on Demand GmbH, Norderstedt Germany
ISBN: 978-3-656-92961-1

**This book at GRIN:**

http://www.grin.com/en/e-book/294717/survey-on-distributed-data-mining-systems

**GRIN - Your knowledge has value**

Since its foundation in 1998, GRIN has specialized in publishing academic texts by students, college teachers and other academics as e-book and printed book. The website www.grin.com is an ideal platform for presenting term papers, final papers, scientific essays, dissertations and specialist books.

**Visit us on the internet:**

http://www.grin.com/

http://www.facebook.com/grincom

http://www.twitter.com/grin_com

# Survey of Distributed Data Mining Systems

Kotagiri Santhosh
University of North Texas

Allam Swetha Reddy
University of North Texas

## ABSTRACT
With the increase in the usage of databases in various fields and domains, to overcome the challenges in a centralized data mining environment, more and more databases are distributed in networks. The objective of distributed data mining is to perform data mining operations based on the type and availability of distributed resources. To make a proper choice of a particular DDM system/model, the basic differences between each of them must be understood. This paper produces a survey of some of the DDM systems available. It mainly focusses on the homogeneous DDM models. It discusses methods based on semantic web and grid, multi-agent, mobile agent and i-Analyst. A hybrid method AGrIP is also discussed. A comparative analysis is made considering different key issues of DDM. Each method is described in detail by its method/algorithm.

## Keywords
DDM; Multi-agent; i-Agent; Ontology; Semantic Web; Grid; CDM; DAP

## 1. INTRODUCTION
Technologies like communication, computation, science are fast growing. They form the fundamental reason for why distributed databases must be used in networks.

Centralized systems are replaced by distributed systems for various reasons; feasibility issues, security issues, limited bandwidth, organizational policies, cross-platform restrictions etc. DDM systems are advantageous over the traditional centralized systems for the following reasons [1]. First, when the model is smaller than the data, transferring the model and not the data will reduce the load on the network. Second, sharing the model is more secure than sharing the data. It also overcomes the security and privacy concerns of any organization. The key issues that determine the performance and utility of any DDM system can be listed [1] as:

- Data Copy: Data from one local site may have to be copied into other sites. The change is one copy not reflecting to the other copy raises the problem of data inconsistency.

- Communication Cost: Unlike in centralized environment where only I/O and CPU cost are considered, communication cost must also be considered in distributed data mining. Bandwidth and amount of data transferred will lead to this communication cost.

- Knowledge Integration: In a distributed scenario, the local results need to be integrated to form the global result. While doing so, the local results are to be verified to match the global degree to avoid ambiguity.

A general distributed data mining architecture is shown in figure 1.

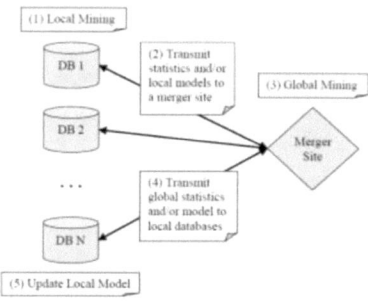

Figure 1: Distributed Data Mining Architecture

The rest of this paper is structured as follows. The classification of different DDM methods and their categorization is explained in section 2. Section 3 discusses in detail some of the homogeneous methods. A comparative analysis is made in section 4. Section 5 concludes the paper.

## 2. Classification of DDM Systems
Out of the many existing DDM systems, few of them are researched and classified into these categories sub categories. A classification hierarchy is shown in figure 2.

### 2.1 Heterogeneous Vs. Homogeneous
Distributed data sources are the partitions of a global virtual data table. These partitions are mined separately. Depending on whether this partition is made horizontally or vertically, DDM systems are classified as heterogeneous or homogeneous [2].

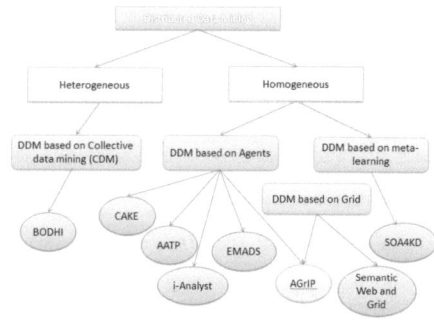

Figure 2: Schematic of DDM techniques

### 2.1.1 Homogeneous DDM systems:
The centralized data mining system is considered homogeneous. All the data are contained in a single DBMS and maintained by a single management model. Everything here is

treated as local. The sub categories of this type of systems are as below. Homogeneous systems are formed when the virtual table is horizontally divided.

### 2.1.1.1 DDM systems based on Data Mining Agents

Data mining agents are like a pseudo program designed to find patterns in data, to pull relevant data, to monitor changes in data etc. Agents have the properties like self-government, smart, Lasting and cooperation [6]. Agents' automation, initiative, collaboration and adaptivity are used to obtain privacy, automation, cooperative mining and dynamic search capability respectively [2]. EMADS, CAKE, i-Analyst, AATP, Mobile Agent based DDM, TREAMA and AOC are some of the models under this category.

### 2.1.1.2 DDM models based on Grid

Grid can be described as a non-interactive work load. It is the sum of all different individual workloads that operate to find a final result. [9] Grid is mainly used for DDM for its advantages like resource sharing, open service and cooperative working. Applications with geographically distributed data use this method for mining. Some of the methods that fall in this category include DataMiningGrid, All Pairs and NORSC. The technology of agent and Grid are combined to form an Agent Grid. This is used to formulate a model named AGrIP.

### 2.1.1.3 Meta-Learning based DDM systems

Meta-learning is coined from the words learning and meta-data. Meta-learning is to learn the performance of the applications applying automatic learning algorithms on meta-data. Some of the methods that belong here are DDM architecture by Tozicka et al. [1,2] using the data source agent for meta-learning, another by Luo et al. by using multi-agents to learn meta-data. Others include SOA4KD, Weka4GML, XCS and EKDTO.

### 2.1.2 Heterogeneous Systems

Dividing the global virtual table vertically gives heterogeneous DDM models. Heterogeneous systems are all based on collective data mining frames (CDM).

### 2.1.2.1 DDM models based on CDM

CDM are used to improve local result quality. It hence reduces the ambiguity in the global results. CDMs give a DDM framework that guarantees correct local analysis and correct aggregation of local data models with minimal data communication. Model that comes under this category is BODHI.

## 3. Methods & Architecture

This section explains some of the methods mentioned above in detail. It concentrates on the agent based methods and Grid based methods.

## 3.1 Extendible Multi Agent Data mining System

Abbreviated as EMADS, this method is a homogeneous DDM technique. EMADS is a multi-agent driven approach and is advantageous over Agent-driven data mining. The architecture of this model is shown in figure 3. EMADS agents are responsible for accessing local data sources and for collaborative data analysis. EMADS includes data mining agents, data agents, task agents, user agents and mediators.

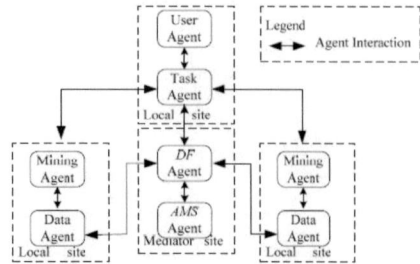

Figure 3: EMADS conceptual framework

The data and mining agents are responsible for accessing data and carrying out the data mining process. These agents work in parallel and share information through the task agent. The task agent coordinates the data mining operations, and presents results to the user agent. Mediators are used for agents' coordination. Data mining is carried out by means of local data mining agents to preserve privacy. Depending on the modes of operation, EMADS can be used by:

- EMADS developers: They develop algorithms
- End Users: Their access is restricted and do data mining tasks
- Contributors: They have restricted access and make the data available for use.

## 3.2 CAKE

CAKE stands for Classifying, Associating & Knowledge Discovery. CAKE uses Parallel Data Mining Agents (PADMAs) [13]. CAKE has a user interface to display the results. The architecture of CAKE is as shown in figure 4.

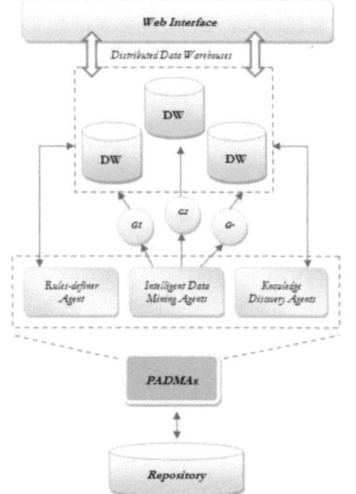

Figure 4: CAKE architecture

It is 4-tier architecture [11] containing:

2

- Distributed data Warehouses: They are physically or logically located on different sites.

- PADMAs: Based on the operation they are of three different categories

  ➢ Rule-definer agents: They are used to define meta-data based on the rules

  ➢ Intelligent Data Mining Agents: They are responsible for all the calculations to mine data and to produce the desired result

  ➢ Knowledge Discovery Agents: They determine the final output to be a success or a failure

### 3.3 i-Analyst based DDM

i-Analyst is an Agent-Based Distributed Data Mining Platform [4]. The architecture shown in figure 5 of i-Analyst can be divided into 2 layers: Resource Management Layer and Execution Layer. Resource management layer is responsible for interacting with users. The modules of this layer include algorithm management used for managing user defined and built-in algorithms, data and visualization management for registering, browsing and viewing data source, project management, case management and instance management for holding other functionalities. Other modules include data mining workflow designer and project report designer.

Second layer is the execution layer called as Distributed Agent Platform (DAP). It comprises of following agents:

- DAP Service Agent (DSA): This agent receives the request, verifies it and sends to CMA

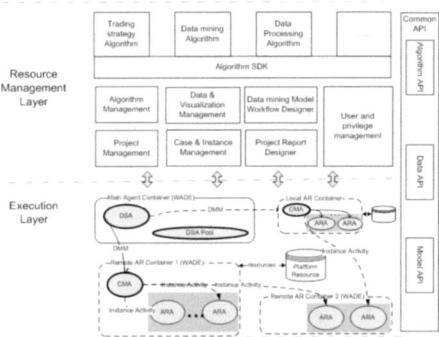

Figure 5: Architecture of i-Analyst

- Case Mediator Agent (CMA): This agent mediates the resources to be local or remote, monitors the execution and notifies DSA results to DSA

- Activity Runner Agent (ARA): ARA is the medium where the action for the actual activity is performed.

### 3.4  Multi Agent DDM model using AATP

AATP stands for Algorithm Analysis and Task Prediction [5]. The architecture of Multi Agent DDM based on AATP is shown in figure 6. It comprises three layers as follows.

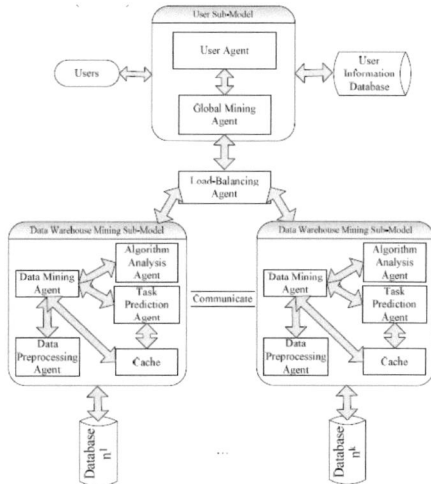

Figure 6: An AATP based Multi-Agent Distributed Data Mining

Service Layer with the support of Data Warehouse Mining sub-model receives requests and mine data. This layer apart from Cache comprises:

- Data Preprocessing Agent: this performs data extraction, cleaning, transformation and simplification.

- Algorithm Analysis Agent: AATP has a built library that provides mining algorithms. This agent is responsible for managing the algorithm lib.

- Data Mining Agent: It performs all the data mining tasks. In this course, it searches cache for other's results and if they are not found, requests the target source agent.

- Task Prediction Agent: This is responsible for minimizing the communication cost. It comes into action when there is a request and feeds them to DMA after prioritizing them

Task Scheduling Layer is implemented by Load Balancing sub model and has LB Agent. It is reasonable for reducing bandwidth. It considers meta-data from DWM model, analyses it and then distributes the tasks. User Interface Layer has two functions. First, the user sends requests through User Agent. It acts as a connection between user and system. Second, this layer combines the User Information DB and Global Mining Agent.

### 3.5  Mobile Agent in DMM

Mobile agent has all the properties as mentioned in section 1. It refers to the task in accordance with the needs of their own from a host of moving to another host is scheduled to be completed [6]. This architecture as shown in figure 7 has 4 different agents.

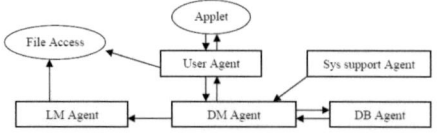

Figure 7: Distributed Data Mining using Mobile Agent

- Data Mining Agent: As the name indicates, it is responsible for all the actions to be performed through data mining tasks
- Support System Agent: it is the provision of the local support to keep itself on a number of local systems.
- Local Management Agent: This is responsible to manage all the security concerns on each of the local system.
- Database Agent: This agent is a mediator between Data Mining agent and User Agent. It interacts with database to get data.
- User Agent: This takes in the request from the user and feeds it to the Data Mining Agent.

### 3.6 DDM based on Semantic Web and Grid

Shown in the figure 8 is the DDM model based on Semantic Web and Grid. This architecture as in the figure 8 consists of 5 layers [8]. All the five layers along with the blocks that comprise them are responsible for the following functions. This architecture introduces a global ontology to solve the problem of semantic heterogeneity- the problem of two local sources having same name but different meaning. It introduces semantic queries and integrates them to the query engine. It also introduces semantic reasoning to directly acquire knowledge. Lastly, Ontology editor is used to add knowledge.

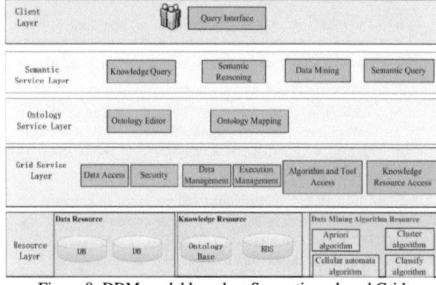

Figure 8: DDM model based on Semantic web and Grid

### 3.7 AGrIP based DDM

In AGrIP [1], A stands for Agent and Gr stands for grid. AGrIP provides infrastructure for Agent based DDM on Grid environment. Figure 9 shows the four layer architecture.

| Applica-tion | E-Science | | Data mining | | | Environment |
|---|---|---|---|---|---|---|
| | | Biology | | E-Business | | |
| Developing Toolkits | Visual Agent Studio | Multi Strategy Minor | Information Retrieval Toolkit | Data Mining Result Visualization | Monitoring Toolkit | Decision Support Toolkit |
| MAGE | Agents providing different kinds of agent grid common services: E.g. GISA provides agent grid information service; DF provides directory service of agent capabilities; GRMA provides management of common resources and services; GSSA provides agent grid security service; DMA: remote data access | | | | | |
| Common Resources | Various resources distributed on Grid: E.g. workstation, personal computer, computer cluster, storage equipment, networks, display devices, databases or datasets, or others, which run on Unix, NT and other operating systems. | | | | | |

Figure 9: Architecture of AGrIP platform

Common resources: consisting of various resources distributed in Grid environment such as workstation, personal computer, computer cluster, storage equipment, databases data sets etc. Agent environment: it is the kernel of Grid computing which is responsible for resource allocation, authentication, communication, task assignment and others. Developing toolkit: providing development environment, containing agent creation, information retrieval, distributed data mining, to let users effectively use Grid resources. Application service: organizing certain agents automatically for specific application purposes.

## 4. COMPARISON & ANALYSIS

Different methods are compared using various parameters and their advantages and weaknesses are listed.

### 4.1 Comparative Analysis:

The comparative analysis of DDM approaches can be done based on the following criteria.

- *Degree of openness*

Degree of openness gives the access restrictions. This refers to the Agent security. The higher the degree of openness, the less is the restriction. Hence, more is the freedom to access data and less is the security.

- *Platform Independence*

A model is said to be platform independent if it can run on different operating systems with consistency. Any model that is based on JAVA can be declared platform independent.

- *Relevance among data sources*

Models should be designed to differentiate similar data sources easily. This will reduce the cost of overall system and also gives efficient results. Semantic difference between data sources must be identified by the model.

- *Quality of final result*

The distributed environment does a plethora of tasks locally and combines them to obtain a global result. The local results must be altered to match the global characteristics while this translation is done. This defines the quality of the final result.

- *Cost of communication*

Cost of communication is present in Distributed data mining models unlike the centralized systems. This must be as minimal as possible for a model to be a better one.

- *Method of Integration*

The local results are to be integrated to form a global result. The method used for this integration should consume very low cost for the model to be a better one.

- *Fault Tolerance*

This is the capacity of a model to achieve recovery from a failure or when a crash occurs [10]. A failure handling mechanism with low execution time for a model would help achieving this.

## 4.2 Different approaches

EMADS is a platform independent model. The limitations for EMADS are that it can only do classification and meta-ARM. In classification with EMADS, agents can be added as this does not hinder the communication overheads. With meta-ARM, EMADS works differently with different algorithms [12].

CAKE uses PADMAs which can work parallel on different things to finish up a task much faster. Therefore it takes less execution time than the rest. This can also help in recovering easily from fault tolerance.

AATP based model has Algorithm Analysis Agent which implements self-learning. This improves the efficiency of this system with time. Also, the Task Prediction Agent reduces the cost of communication.

i-Analyst based DDM technique uses multi agent collaboration. This outperforms single agent approach. The experiments on this approach show that agents are used to boost the performance and enable distribution of data and execution on a high level.

Mobile Agent approach though consumes high cost of communication, gives efficient solutions to DDM. This system can be improved by adding fault tolerance agents and r decreasing the cost of communication.

In Semantic web and Grid DDM method, Semantic web technology solves the heterogeneity of data sources and the Grid architecture provides efficient data analysis and high result quality.

## 4.3 Challenges

The key challenges [2] faced by the current DDM methods are:

- Result Quality: Methods if found for measuring semantic difference and relations, modifying DDM pattern and integration methods would improve the quality of the final result

- DDM efficiency: Cost of communication must be minimized and the load must be balanced well among sources

## 5. CONCLUSION

This paper displays a survey of existing Distributed Data Mining techniques and summarizes a few of the homogeneous methods. It showcases a comparative analysis mentioning the advantages and disadvantages of each of the methods. The further work could include extending the survey to methods like cloud computing [11] combined with DDM and expanding the analysis to other comparison dimensions.

## 6. REFERENCES

[1] Bin Liu, Shu-Gui Cao, Xiao-Li Jia and Zhao-Hua Zhi, "Data mining in ditributed data environment", Machine Learning and Cybernetics (ICMLC), 2010 International Conference, Vol. 1, 421 - 426.

[2] Bin Liu, Shu-Gui Cao, Xiao-Li Jia and Zhao-Hua Zhi, "A hierarchical distributed data mining architecture", Machine Learning and Cybernetics (ICMLC), 2010 International Conference, Vol. 1, 40 - 44.

[3] Xianglei Meng and Deyu Dang, "A Model for Parallel Data Mining Based on Multi-Agent", Wireless Communications, Networking and Mobile Computing, 2009. WiCom '09. 5th International Conference, Page(s): 1 - 4

[4] Chayapol Moemeng, Xinhua Zhu, Longbing Cao and Chen Jiahang, " i-Analyst: An Agent-Based Distributed Data Mining Platform", Data Mining Workshops (ICDMW), 2010 IEEE International Conference. Page(s): 1404 - 1406

[5] Dan Zhou, Wenbi Rao and Fangsu Lv, "A Multi-Agent Distributed Data Mining Model Based on Algorithm Analysis and Task Prediction", Information Engineering and Computer Science (ICIECS), 2010 2nd International Conference, Pages(s): 1 - 4

[6] Ma Yubao and Ding Renyuan, "Mobile Agent Technology and Its Application in Distributed Data Mining", Database Technology and Applications, 2009 First International Workshop, Page(s):: 151 – 155

[7] Pathak, B. and Sinha, M., "Analytical study of agent based distributed data mining and its ontology", Computing for Sustainable Global Development (INDIACom), 2014 International Conference, Page(s): 400 – 404

[8] Huimin Wang, Nie Guihua and Kui Fu, "Distributed Data Mining Based on Semantic Web and Grid", Computational Intelligence and Natural Computing, 2009. CINC '09. International Conference, Page(s): Vol. 2, 232 – 234

[9] Ning Zhang and Bao Hong, "Research on Distributed Data Mining Technology Based on Grid", Database Technology and Applications, 2009 First International Workshop, Page(s): 440 - 443.

[10] Cesario, E. and Talia, D., "A Failure Handling Framework for Distributed Data Mining Services on the Grid", Parallel, Distributed and Network-Based Processing (PDP), 2011 19th Euromicro International Conference, Page(s): 70 – 79

[11] Othmane, B. and Hebri, R.S.A., "Cloud computing & multi-agent systems: A new promising approach for distributed data mining", Information Technology Interfaces (ITI), Proceedings of the ITI 2012 34th International Conference, Page(s): 111 – 116

[12] Kamal Ali Albashiri and Frans Coenen, "The EMADS Extendible Multi-Agent DataMining Framework", Data Mining and Multi-agent Integration (2009), Page(s): 8 – 12

[13] Danish Khan, "CAKE – Classifying, Associating & Knowledge Discovery. An Approach for Distributed Data Mining (DDM) using Parallel Data Mining Agents (PADMAs)", 2008 IEEE/WIC/ACM International Conference on Web Intelligence and Intelligent Agent Technology, Page(s): 596- 601